THE HOUSE BY THE STABLE

A CHRISTMAS PLAY

BY
CHARLES WILLIAMS

Copyright © 2018 Read Books Ltd.
This book is copyright and may not be
reproduced or copied in any way without
the express permission of the publisher in writing

British Library Cataloguing-in-Publication Data
A catalogue record for this book is available from
the British Library

A HISTORY OF THE THEATRE

'The Theatre' is a collaborative form of fine art that uses live performers to present the experience of a real or imagined event. The performers may communicate this experience to the audience through combinations of gesture, speech, song, music, and dance, with elements of art, stagecraft and set design used to enhance the physicality, presence and immediacy of the experience. The specific place of the performance is also named by the word 'theatre' – derived from the Ancient Greek word *théatron*, meaning 'a place for viewing', itself from *theáomai*, meaning 'to see', 'watch' or 'observe'.

Modern Western theatre largely derives from ancient Greek drama, from which it borrows technical terminology, classification into genres, and many of its themes, stock characters, and plot elements. The city-state of Athens is where 'theatre' as we know it originated, as part of a broader culture of theatricality and performance in classical Greece that included festivals, religious rituals, politics, law, athletics, music, poetry, weddings, funerals, and symposia. Participation in the city-state's many festivals – and attendance at the City Dionysia as an audience member (or even as a participant in the theatrical productions) in particular, was an important part of citizenship.

The theatre of ancient Greece consisted of three types of drama: tragedy, comedy, and the satyr play (a form of tragicomedy, similar in spirit to the bawdy satire of burlesque). The origins of theatre in ancient Greece, according to Aristotle (384–322 BCE), the first theoretician of theatre, are to be found in the festivals that honoured Dionysus. These performances (the aforementioned City Dionysia) were held in semi-circular auditoria cut into hillsides, capable of seating 10,000–20,000 people. The stage consisted of a dancing floor (orchestra), dressing room and scene-building area (skene). Since the words were the most important part, good acoustics and clear delivery were paramount. The actors (always men) wore masks appropriate to the characters they represented, and each might play several parts.

Athenian tragedy (the oldest surviving form of tragedy) emerged sometime during the sixth century BCE, and flowered during the fifth century BCE – from the end of which it began to spread throughout the Greek world – and continued in popularity until the beginning of the Hellenistic period. Aeschylus, Sophocles, and Euripides were masters of the genre. The other side of the coin – Athenian comedy, is conventionally divided into three periods; 'Old Comedy', 'Middle Comedy', and 'New Comedy'. Old Comedy survives today largely in the form of the eleven surviving plays of Aristophanes, while Middle Comedy is largely lost (preserved only in a few relatively short fragments in authors such as Athenaeus of Naucratis). New Comedy is known primarily from the substantial papyrus fragments of Menander.

Western theatre developed and expanded considerably under the Romans. The theatre of ancient Rome was a thriving and diverse art form, ranging from festival performances of street theatre, nude dancing, and acrobatics, to the staging of Plautus's broadly appealing situation comedies, to the high-style, verbally elaborate tragedies of Seneca. Although Rome had a native tradition of performance, the Hellenization of Roman culture in the third century BCE had a profound and energizing effect on Roman theatre and encouraged the development of Latin literature of the highest quality for the stage. This tradition fed into the modern theatre we know today, and during the renaissance, theatre generally moved away from the poetic drama of the Greeks, and towards a more naturalistic prose style of dialogue. By the nineteenth century and the Industrial Revolution, this trend continued to progress.

In England, theatre was immensely popular, but took a big pause during 1642 and 1660 because of Cromwell's Interregnum. Prior to this, 'English renaissance theatre' was witnessed, with celebrated playwrights such as William Shakespeare, Christopher Marlowe and Ben Jonson. Under Queen Elizabeth, drama was a unified expression as far as social class was concerned, and the Court watched the same plays the commoners saw in the public playhouses. With the development of the private theatres, drama became more oriented towards the tastes and values of an upper-class audience however. By the later part of the reign of Charles I, few new plays were being written for the public theatres, which sustained themselves on the accumulated works of the previous decades. Theatre was now seen as something sinful and the Puritans tried very hard to drive it out of their society. Due to this stagnant period, once Charles II came back to the throne in 1660, theatre (among other arts) exploded with influences from France, and the wider continent.

The eighteenth century saw the widespread introduction of women to the stage – a development previously unthinkable. These women were looked at as celebrities (also a newer concept, thanks to ideas on individualism that were beginning to be born in Renaissance Humanism) but on the other hand, it was still very new and revolutionary. Comedies were full of the young and very much in vogue, with the storyline following their love lives: commonly a young roguish hero professing his love to the chaste and free minded heroine near the end of the play, much like Sheridan's *The School for Scandal*. Many of the comedies were fashioned after the French tradition, mainly Molière (the great comedic playwright), again harking back to the French influence of the King and his court after their exile.

After this point, there was an explosion of theatrical styles. Throughout the nineteenth century, the popular theatrical forms of Romanticism, melodrama, Victorian burlesque and the well-made plays of Scribe and Sardou gave way to the problem plays of Naturalism and Realism; the farces of Feydeau; Wagner's operatic *Gesamtkunstwerk*; musical theatre (including Gilbert and Sullivan's operas); F. C. Burnand's, W. S. Gilbert's and Wilde's drawing-room comedies; Symbolism; proto-Expressionism in the late works of August Strindberg and Henrik Ibsen; and Edwardian musical comedy. The list continues! These trends continued through the twentieth century in the realism of Stanislavski and Lee Strasberg, the political theatre of Erwin Piscator and Bertolt Brecht, the so-called Theatre of the Absurd of Samuel Beckett and Eugène Ionesco, and the rise of American and British musicals.

Theatre itself has an incredibly long history, and despite the massive proliferation of theatrical styles and mediums – it essentially owes its existence to the ancient Greeks and the Romans. The three main genres; tragedy, comedy and satyre, continue to influence plot themes, directing, writing and acting, with frequent and fascinating interrelations and overlaps. As a genre, it remains as popular today as it has ever been, and continues as a massive influence on popular culture more broadly. It is hoped that the current reader enjoys this book on the subject.

CHARLES WILLIAMS

Charles Walter Stansby Williams was born in London in 1886. He dropped out of University College London in 1904, and was hired by Oxford University Press as a proof-reader, quickly rising to the position of editor. While there, arguably his greatest editorial achievement was the publication of the first major English-language edition of the works of the Danish philosopher Søren Kierkegaard.

Williams began writing in the twenties and went on to publish seven novels. Of these, the best-known are probably *War in Heaven* (1930), *Descent into Hell* (1937), and *All Hallows' Eve* (1945) – all fantasies set in the contemporary world. He also published a vast body of well-received scholarship, including a study of Dante entitled *The Figure of Beatrice* (1944) which remains a standard reference text for academics today, and a highly unconventional history of the church, *Descent of the Dove* (1939). Williams garnered a number of well-known admirers, including T. S. Eliot, W. H. Auden and C. S. Lewis. Towards the end of his life, he gave lectures at Oxford University on John Milton, and received an honorary MA degree. Williams died almost exactly at the close of World War II, aged 58.

CHARACTERS

MAN
PRIDE
HELL
GABRIEL
JOSEPH
MARY

The Scene is in Man's house on the one side and in its stable on the other

THE HOUSE BY THE STABLE

Enter MAN *and* PRIDE

PRIDE. What, are you not tired? will you still walk?
  will you still talk of me and of us and of you?
MAN. I desire nothing better now, and nothing new.[1]
  It was a high and happy day when we met.
  Will you never forget it? and love me always?
PRIDE.   Yes:
  I will love you always.
MAN.   So I believe indeed,
  and feed on the thought—to be everlastingly loved.
  Tell me, how did this surprise come true?
PRIDE. It is no surprise—if you think what you are.
  Indeed, it were stranger if I adored you less.
  You are Man, the lord of this great house Earth,
  or (as its name is called in my country) Sin;
  you are its god and mine; since you first smiled
  and stretched your hand to me and brought me in,
  since our tenderness began, I have loved you, Man,
  and will—do not doubt; kiss me again.
MAN. You are my worshipful sweet Pride; will you be
  so arrogant always to others and humble to me?
  Will you always make me believe in myself? I am Man,
  but before you came, Pride, I was half-afraid
  that someone or something had been before me, and made
  me and my house, and could ruin or cast aside.
  But when I look in your dove's eyes, Pride,
  and see myself there, I know I am quite alone
  in my greatness, and all that I have is quite my own.
PRIDE. So this wonderful house where moon and sun

---

[1] These first three lines may be omitted when a curtain is available.

run with lights, and all kinds of creatures crawl
to be your servants, and your only business is to take
delight in your own might—it is yours and mine,
a shrine for your godhead, and for me because I am yours.
MAN. Thus endures my love for my own Pride.
To thrust you out were to doubt myself; that
is a bygone folly now—I will do so no more.
PRIDE. No; do not: be content to love me.
See, to teach you (let me pretend awhile
that I can add something to your style—I
who am also and only your creature) I have brought here
my brother, born of one nature with me, my twin,
or a moment younger: let me call him in,
and he shall tell you more of what I have planned.
                                        [*Enter* HELL
MAN. Are you my Pride's brother? give me your hand.
We must be friends; tell me, what is your name?
HELL. I am called Hell.
MAN.   And where, Hell, do you live?
HELL. Why, as to that, it is not easy to give
a clear definition of the place; it is not far
as your journeys go, and no bar to finding,
but the minding of the way is best found by going,
and that (of all means) best at my sister's showing.
MAN. We will go there some time.
PRIDE.   O soon, sweet Man, soon—
for, I must tell you, I have begged of my brother a boon,
first because you are my sweetheart, and next
because the laws you have made everywhere mean
you should have all the best. This is a brave
house you live in—and let me call it Sin,
because my tongue trips if I name it Earth—
but my brother in his country has a house braver still
and has promised it to us, of his own kind will.

MAN. Aye, has he? that is noble, and yet he knows
   perhaps I would take it from him, would he not,
   and I saw it one day and chose to have it for mine.
PRIDE. O love, how I love to hear you talk so!
   but for my sake do not be harsh to my brother;
   for your Pride's sake, smile at her brother Hell,
   and treat him well.
MAN.　　　　　　Why, that I will do.
   How now, Hell, shall I have a house from you?
   Tell me of it.
HELL.　　　　It is strong and very old,
   but (by a burning I have made there) never cold,
   and dry—the only damp would be your tears
   if Man could ever weep. The air provokes
   hunger often—you are so sharp-set
   you could almost eat yourself. The view is wide—
   heavenly, as men say in your tongue, to the other side
   of the sky at least, so far it seems away,
   and whatever is there will never interfere;
   that is quite certain. Because my sister desires
   I will give you this house if you choose.
MAN.　　　　　　　　And because my thews
   are strong enough to take it too perhaps?
HELL. That also, no doubt.
MAN.　　　　　　Well, let that be.
   You are a good fellow, Hell; you shall live there
   whenever you like, even if you give it to me.
   The three of us could be royal in such a house.
   We will have a drink on it first.
　　　　　　　　　　　[*He goes to fetch wine*
HELL [*to* PRIDE]. Have you seen the jewel yet?
PRIDE [*to* HELL].　　　　　　　　No chance;
   I think he has forgotten where it is himself.
HELL [*to* PRIDE]. What have you been doing all this while?

THE HOUSE BY THE STABLE

PRIDE [*to* HELL].   Hush!
   I have a trick now; play to my lead.
MAN [*pouring out the wine*]. This is good wine; I have had it in
   store
   more than I could guess; it improves with every flask.
   None could ask better. I must have tended the vines
   when I was young; there are no vines now
   or few: I have sometimes thought—were it not for my smile
   over it—the land would be more sterile than it was.
   Here; drink. You must need that.
PRIDE [*to* MAN].   Sweet,
   for Pride's sake throw him something in return,
   some trifle; I would not have my lord
   seem under an obligation even to Hell
   my brother—though indeed I meant well enough
   in persuading him.
MAN.   You are always right; no kindness
   but I am always just to pay it back.
   Now, brother, you must take something—yes,
   no words; I say you must. What will you have?
   Pride, what shall I give him?
PRIDE.   If you would be
   kind, play a game of dice—the best of three:
   it would please him; he loves a gamble.
MAN.   Dice? good.
   What shall we play for?
PRIDE.   Something quite small,
   or even nothing at all; the game is the thing.
MAN. No; something I will chance in return for a house.
   What?
                                                             [*He drinks*
PRIDE. A handful of dust of your own—Earth;
   or—if you want, as becomes you, to risk more—
   say that old jewel your servant talks

THE HOUSE BY THE STABLE

often of—more often than becomes him.
Soul, he calls it, I think.

MAN. Soul? yes;
truly he does talk thus; but if
ever such a thing was, it has been tossed
one day away in a corner of the house and lost.
Besides, I have heard him sing sometimes of a bird
that sat in the leaves of paradise and sang,
and in his song he calls that bird Soul.
I do not know; my paradise is I,
and any soul that sings in me I will try
on the dice any time.

[*He drinks*
Look at me, Pride; you will be
always faithful, will you not?

PRIDE. Always, by my will.

MAN. I would kill you else.

PRIDE. I am not easy to kill
by any who have loved me. Sweet, we forget my brother.
Come, let us risk this lost jewel your soul
on the dice, let Hell have his chance of finding.

[*Enter* GABRIEL

GABRIEL. Sir, by permission; there are poor people outside
seeking shelter.

PRIDE. Insolence!

MAN. Who?

GABRIEL. One
from these parts, a youngish working man,
and has his heart's love with him, his wife,
a fair-faced girl, and (I think) near her time.
It is a harsh night; if I may suggest
she needs immediate rest—a room, and a bed.

PRIDE. Man, this servant of yours clacks his tongue
more freely than mine should do; must you keep

THE HOUSE BY THE STABLE

rooms where any riff-raff tramps may sleep—
and have supper too, I suppose? you, sir,
I am speaking to you.
GABRIEL. And supper, madam, you suppose.
HELL. Hey, you, speak well to your lord's guest,
my sister, or. . . .
GABRIEL [*angelically*]. Or. . .?
MAN. Rest quiet, Hell:
I have had this fellow for servant a long time,
ever since before I came hither, wherever
I was before I came hither; he suits.
He is neat and quick and keeps out of the way,
and looks after my accounts—at least someone does,
and it isn't I; let him alone.

[*He drinks*

GABRIEL. Will you choose, sir, to speak to them yourself?
MAN. Why . . . it were wrong to turn a mother away
and pity to turn a woman, on a hard night,
in a plight of that kind; but tramps in my rooms . . . yet
one should be tender when one is comfortable, sweet,
tender to the poor, yes?
PRIDE. I confess, dear Man,
I cannot see why; one cannot do what one would—
no, not you even, my bountiful god—
and (as things go) they are only encouraged to expect
more than anyone can do. My darling, have a care.
MAN. Well, there is that . . .
GABRIEL. I think, sir,
you should see them now.
MAN. Do you? Well . . . well,
just for a moment then; let them come in.
You are always ready to beguile me. And as for you,
Hell and my sweet Pride, be merry the while.

[GABRIEL *goes out.* MAN *drinks*

THE HOUSE BY THE STABLE

HELL [*to* PRIDE]. Surely that is Gabriel, that old gossip of heaven?
PRIDE [*to* HELL]. He? I cannot tell; angels and I
    never met much, not for me to recognize.
HELL [*to* PRIDE]. Your dove's eyes are not so sharp as mine.
    I have peered more deeps than you; besides, sleep
    takes you sometimes; it never takes me,
    and after a while he who wakes for ever
    finds the tingling and aching make sight the sharper
    in the land where the heart-breaking troubles the light.
    I am sure it is Gabriel; wait; show no sign—
    only be ready to whisper Man a little
    and keep your eye on the door.
PRIDE [*to* HELL]. Why, what can he do?
HELL [*to* PRIDE]. I do not know; nothing, I hope; if Man
    chooses to play, it is his affair and mine.
    But keep close; we may win the jewel yet,
    and Man get clear with us to my nice house.

                                              [*He sniggers*

PRIDE. Come, if you will see them, let us drink first!
MAN. Gabriel might have brought me more wine first.
    The curst fellow! he must be taught his job,
    and not to rob me of time for wandering tramps.
    Well, I have promised this time. Here, now
    let us drink to our union—
HELL.   Eternal, eternal!

                    [GABRIEL *brings in* JOSEPH *and* MARY

GABRIEL. Here, sir, they are.
MAN.   What do you want?
JOSEPH. Sir, shelter for one night, by your permission.
    Our mule has gone lame; the dark overtook us
    and all but shook our hearts with perils of the road.
    My wife is in no condition to go on.
    To-morrow we will be gone.

MAN.   Poor wretch!
She needs a fetch of care.
PRIDE.   Beware, sweet.
It is easier to let them in than to get them out.
You are too kind. Besides, if you have a mind
to go on this journey with our brother Hell,
you do not want strangers to rack your house
when your back is turned: anyone as great as you
must be true to his glory.
MAN.   She is a poor lass.
PRIDE. That is why; if she were of our class—
not yours; you are non-pareil—but my brother's and mine . . .
but do as you think best!
MAN.   For a night's rest . . .
PRIDE. To have people like these in the house—imagine!
But you, I know, are their master—and mine.
I am only thinking of your glory.
MAN.   Well, yes;
I see that . . . Gabriel!
GABRIEL.   Sir!
MAN.   Think:
is there no shed near where these could be stored
for a night in reasonable comfort? I can't afford
to have them inside; my Pride will not stomach it,
and yet I am loth to push them both outside
till their plight is a little better.
GABRIEL.   The stable, sir:
it is empty since you chose to dispose of your stud.
MAN. Good: give them a shake-down of straw there:
   [*Half-aside to* GABRIEL] and hark! if you care to hand them a
     hunch of bread
I shall look the other way.
                                              [*He drinks*

THE HOUSE BY THE STABLE

GABRIEL. Sir, it is God's bread.
I will do as you say.
MAN. O God, God!
Why must you always bring your fairy-tales in?
Did God build this great house Sin?
Did God send this pleasant leman Pride?
What has God ever done for Man?
GABRIEL. He gave that jewel your soul.
MAN. O soul!
This is your old clack, Gabriel. In the whole
of my vast property I never found it anywhere—
with flesh, fish, or fowl. It must needs be some old
hidaway rubbish. And what is God doing,
if God is, being bounteous to me?
For anything I can see, I had neither God
nor father on earth: I was always just Man
since the world began. You tire me; go,
get them away.
GABRIEL. Sir, just as you say.
JOSEPH. Sir, a blessing on you for this grace!
Thank him, Mary.
MARY. Sir, God will bless you;
nor will my Son, when he comes, forget
what you gave nor with what spirit. If
he can be ever of use to you, I vow
now, in his name, he will be well content to be.
MAN. You are heartily welcome. Gabriel, have them away.
 [GABRIEL *takes them across to the stable*
There, they are gone: now we can drink again.
Pour it out, Hell. Pride, give me your hand;
am I not a grand fellow?
PRIDE. Sir, just as you say!
Nay, I love you, dear Man, for being so fine,

THE HOUSE BY THE STABLE

so full of your own importance. Do you not find
me more to your mind than a girl like that?

[*While they dally,* GABRIEL *covers the Nativity, and the three sing the Magnificat, which* PRIDE *interrupts at the following points*]

MARY. My soul doth magnify the Lord, and my spirit hath rejoiced in God my Saviour, for he hath regarded the low estate of his handmaiden: for, behold, from henceforth all generations shall call me blessed.

PRIDE. Henceforth, we shall be the only blessed ones on earth; and no generations of anything except our joy.

MARY. For he that is mighty hath done to me great things; and holy is his name. And his mercy is on them that fear him from generation to generation. He hath showed strength with his arm; . . .

PRIDE. Be my arm of strength, Man.

MARY. . . . he hath scattered the proud in the imagination of their hearts.

PRIDE. Imagine me in your heart.

MARY. He hath put down the mighty from their seats, and exalted them of low degree.

PRIDE. Be mighty on me; exalt me to your great degree.

MARY. He hath filled the hungry with good things; and the rich he hath sent empty away.

PRIDE. O rich, rich!—bear off, my dear;
no, my brother is here. Tower—will you?—
over me in your power? O but fling him too
your glory's world's wealth! let all my house
go down before your head's crown of splendour.
Tender us all our desires out of your greatness:
to him his gambling moment, his catch of chance;
then snatch me to yourself for ever.
Then, at the gate of your house, when we go

THE HOUSE BY THE STABLE

I will kiss you so ... do you know? wait, my sweet!
Hell, have you the dice?
MAN.   I have dice here.
I used them often enough when I played with my friends,
but since I met you I have forgotten my friends.
Love of you tends to that.
HELL.   Do we play for a stake?
I do not mind; the game is enough.
PRIDE.   Yes:
but a stake, all the same, makes the game more amusing.
And, brother, you forget—you play for that jewel
called soul.
MAN.   Why, it does not exist, or if,
you will never find it.
PRIDE.   It will do; it is in my mind
that to play for the chance to find it is well enough.
What do you say, Hell?
HELL.   Aye; if I have his will
to lay hold of it, if I can, by my own skill—
nothing unfair, no force; but if it is found,
I take it in free exchange for the house and ground.
MAN. You shall, brother, for your sister's sake and yours.
HELL. However precious?
MAN.   Though it were worth my all.
                                        [*He drinks*
I am no miser; I was always open-handed—
was I not, Pride my lass? give me a kiss
and I shall win the game and my soul as well.
Two out of three; throw.
                                        [*They play*
HELL.   Five.
MAN.   Six. Ha,
that is my gain. Kiss me again, Pride.

THE HOUSE BY THE STABLE

PRIDE [*to* HELL]. Quick now, while he is blind with me.
  [*While they kiss* HELL *changes the dice*
MAN. Well tossed, Hell; you have a knack, but my luck
  is in now, and I back my luck to win.
  [*He drinks*
GABRIEL. Man, where are you?
MAN. Who was that called?
PRIDE. No one.
HELL. The wind.
MAN. It was a voice of some kind.
  [*He looks out*
  The rain is over; the stars are out; one
  over the stable is more sun than star.
PRIDE. How slow you are! Man, your Pride is waiting.
MAN [*he is now rather drunk*]. Waiting, is she? let her wait then.
  Why, you hussy, you are a part of me.
  I am not to be called in as if I were Gabriel
  to be scolded at pleasure.
PRIDE. No; it was but that leisure
  of ours, in Hell's house, I was wanting . . . but so,
  just as you say.
MAN. Ha, yes: again.
  To it again.
  [*He throws*
  Five.
  [HELL *throws*
HELL. Six.
MAN. What tricks . . . ? let me see. Six: it is—you have won.
  [*He roars with laughter*
  Ho, this is a fine thing we have done—
  drawn the game.
HELL. No; one throw more.
MAN. More? how many times have we thrown?

THE HOUSE BY THE STABLE

HELL. Twice.
   Hurry!
MAN. What, hurry? what do you mean?
   you are as saucy as this quean herself.
HELL. Throw; I am impatient for you to go.
MAN. Do you hear that, Pride? he wants us to go.
   He wants to hunt for my soul.
                      [*He roars again with laughter*
PRIDE. No.
   I do not think he will long hunt for that.
MAN. Well, kiss me—a kiss hearty and strong,
   better than before; give me the winning throw.
                   [*She leans over and kisses him lazily*
JOSEPH. Man, Man, where are you?
MAN. Aye! . . . here.
   Who wants Man?
PRIDE *and* HELL. No one; no one; throw.
MAN. Someone wanted; someone called; who?
PRIDE [*seizing his hand*]. Throw—with me, thus; and I with you.
MAN. Let me go. I am Man; I will not be forced.
   I will have you horsed on your brother's back, my girl,
   and take such a cudgel to you as will crack
   some of those pretty bones.
PRIDE [*to* HELL]. Throw first,
   and he afterwards; or at the very worst
   we will persuade him he threw and lost the game.
HELL [*throwing*]. Six.
MARY. Man, where are you?
MAN. That was the girl;
   that was the pretty wife—hey, now
   I am coming, Man is coming.
PRIDE *and* HELL [*seizing him*]. No; throw.
MAN. What is this? what is happening? How
   do I hear a voice I have not chosen to hear

outside my house? Who made my house?
There was no one, was there?
PRIDE.   No.
HELL.   No.
MAN.   Then how
do I hear the voice of something outside me?
Or is one of you playing a trick on me? Pride,
if I thought . . . I am caught . . . my mind is twined in a voice . . .
it isn't yours . . . whose is it? Ho, you,
Gabriel!
HELL.   No; leave Gabriel alone.
PRIDE. Sweet, sweet Man, leave Gabriel alone.
MAN. No; Gabriel is my fellow; he will help.
He was here before I came hither; he suits.
He will tell me the voices. Gabriel, Gabriel, I say!
GABRIEL [*coming across in his magnificence*]. Here!
Sir, God made me and bade me wait
on this moment in your life: what do you need?
MAN. You are a good fellow: come here: listen.
My brother Hell and my leman Pride mean
to have me finish . . . that was not it neither;
there was something else . . . the girl, Gabriel, the girl.
I heard her call out: where is she?
Is she in danger?
GABRIEL.   No; she is quite safe.
This is the game, sir, is it?
                    [*He picks up one of the dice and looks at it*
PRIDE [*to* HELL]. Fool, you have tried too many ways to get him.
HELL [*to* PRIDE]. Damn him, who would have thought grace was
   so near
as to hear that small squeak of a drunken voice?
MAN [*sleepily*]. The game, yes—but I don't know where we were.
Throw for me . . . the girl is safe, is she?
and her baby . . . hadn't she got a baby?

THE HOUSE BY THE STABLE

GABRIEL. She has.
   Now.
MAN. Yes ... to be sure. ... Pride ... Pride,
   where are you?

                                                    [*He dozes off*
PRIDE. Here, darling, here.
GABRIEL [*catching her by the hair and pulling her back*]. Peace:
   let the poor fellow sleep a little; you
     would never be caught by anything as natural as drink.
HELL. Let her go. What are you doing there with my dice?
GABRIEL [*tossing the dice in the air and catching it*]. Dice—ha! So:
   that is better.
   It seems now to have only one six:
   and now we can play the last throw again.
HELL [*whining*]. I won't! I tell you I won't! I won't play.
PRIDE [*snarling*]. Don't you, Hell: the nasty-minded scut,
   pretending we cheated.

       [GABRIEL *takes each of them by an ear, and knocks their
       heads lightly together*]
PRIDE. Oo! don't—you hurt!
       [*She drops to the floor, moaning and rubbing her head*
GABRIEL. You wanted the game; you shall win or lose on the game
   by the luck of the game, but all luck is good.
   Toil and spoil as you will, still in the end
   the flick of every chance must fall right.
   Throw.
HELL. I don't ...
GABRIEL [*terribly*]. Throw.

                                                [HELL *throws*
                  Five.
                                              [GABRIEL *throws*
                 Speak—
   what is it?
HELL [*cowering*]. Six.

THE HOUSE BY THE STABLE

GABRIEL. You have had a long run,
you and all your tricks, but to-morrow's sun
rises on a world where untruth is always untrue.
That is simple enough but too difficult for you.
Get to your house and the burning you made—and not even
that is your own; the fire is borrowed from heaven.
            [HELL *goes*
And as for you, sister, you poor cheap
cowardly shrew; you . . .
    [*With an awful angelic effort he restrains himself*
I will teach you one lesson; kneel up; say after me:
         [*She obeys. He puts on his glory*
Glory to God in the highest, and on earth peace:
goodwill to men.
       [PRIDE *repeats the words, snivelling*
And now go.
          [*She begins to get up*
  No; on your knees: go.
           [*She shuffles away*
MAN [*waking*]. I dreamt my Pride had gone.
           [*He stares round*
Where is she? what has been happening? call her, you,
Gabriel.
GABRIEL. Sir, soon, if you tell me to.
They will wait, I know, by the gate you call Death,
which is the usual way to Hell's house.
You may catch them there or yourself call them back.
But there is a thing to do before you go.
MAN. What? do you bully me? I want my Pride;
I want to be a god; she made a vow
never to leave me.
GABRIEL.   Nor did she—to be just.
It was I—for this single night—made her go.
MAN. You are above yourself.

16

THE HOUSE BY THE STABLE

GABRIEL.   Above or beside—
distinct enough at least to deal with Pride.
There is a thing that you must see to-night
of your own sight, without Pride's arms round you
or Hell's hand in yours. This one hour
out of all time is given you to see it yourself.
To-morrow things may change. The woman you saved
half by your will from a little chill in the night,
and from blistered feet, has a word to say. Come.
MAN. It seems I made her a poor offer, yet
she was better in the straw than in the street:
do you not think so? You look grander than you used.
GABRIEL. Sir, it is only that you give me more attention.
When Pride is about, no one can see straight.
You shall see more than I. Come when I call.
                                      [*He goes to the stable*
JOSEPH. Blessed one, what is your will now?
MARY. Dearest lord, to show Man my child;
lest in some testy humour the rumour should fade.
If he sees, his heart may radically move to love,
whatever he forgets, wherever he sets his eyes.
JOSEPH. He who with all this Earth offered us the straw?
MARY. Did we deserve, dearest, under the law,
this birth that I kiss? Nothing at all is given
till all is given, I know; that is heaven.
But then also it is heaven to know that all
is given at once in the smallest free gift—
even sometimes when only half-given. O my Son
reckons as no arithmetician has done;
he checks his amounts by the least and the greatest at once.
O my Own, there are no, no accounts like yours!
JOSEPH. Blessed is he in his sole free choice!
GABRIEL. Lady, Man is a little drunk, and a little
sleepy, with a little hankering after hell,

THE HOUSE BY THE STABLE

but yet also he has a faint hurt
at having offered as he did; if it pleased you now
to expose the Holy Thing—
MARY.   O let him come!
let him come quickly!
GABRIEL.   Man! Man!
                                      [MAN *stumbles across*
MAN. It is almost too bright here to see. Where
is the lady? I did give her a hunch of bread
and a place to lie; she might else have been dead.
JOSEPH. Do not talk nonsense.
GABRIEL.   Do not talk at all.
MAN. No, but I am trying to understand: why
should I who had one house, and another beyond
promised, have been so fond as to offer straw
in a stable? and yet . . .
GABRIEL.   Do not trouble your brain;
gain is as difficult to understand as grace.
JOSEPH. Do not talk, I say, lest the Divine One sleep.
MARY. Nay, let him talk as he will; he is mine; come,
Man my friend; it is true that but for you
I might have come to an end—here, at least.
                                  [*She gives him her hand*
Look, my Son thanks you.
MAN.   Was he born here?
MARY. This very night, in your stable; therefore, dear Man,
you, if you choose, shall be his god-father.
MAN. What will you call him, lady?
MARY   Jesus, because
he shall presently save his people from their sins—
and Hell shall play no trick on them more.
MAN. I did not quite refuse you, did I? or did I?
I cannot tell; Hell has made me stupid.
Did I deny you all or did I not?

THE HOUSE BY THE STABLE

Look now, he must have something to please him.
The house is full of things, and none right.
Stop; I remember something out of sight,
out of thought, but always I have had round my neck.
    [*He fumbles at his breast and pulls out a jewel*
There; it was once bright; it might serve.
I do not know what it is at all.
But if you should want a bed for the rest of the night,
there is my room the best.
GABRIEL.   But this is your soul
I have searched for all this time!
MARY [*laughing up at him*]. Great Hierarch, even
the angels desire to understand these things,
and a mortal hand does more than the Domination.
Leave Man and my Son and me our mystery;
let us think our own way and not yours.
Look, I will breathe on it—so, and see
how it dances, and how my Beloved's glances follow.
Take it again, Man, a little while;
we will go up to your room.
    [GABRIEL *and* JOSEPH *help her to rise*
    Now be the gloom
of earth split, and be this house blest
and no more professed by poor Pride to be Sin,
for the joys of love hereafter shall over-ride
boasting and bragging and the heavy lagging of Hell
after delight that outstrips him—step and sight.
   [*She makes the sign of the Cross towards the house*
Take us, O exchange of hearts! this we know—
substance is love, love substance. Let us go.
      [*They go out*

www.ingramcontent.com/pod-product-compliance
Lightning Source LLC
Chambersburg PA
CBHW022129090426
42743CB00008B/1072